The Polka Dot Chair

Other Books by Michele Heeney

My Paper Children (2008)
Keep the Change (2009)
The Monkey Tree (2010)

Michele Heeney

The Polka Dot Chair
New and Selected Poems

With Photographs by the Author

Terra Nova Books
SANTA FE, NEW MEXICO

Terra Nova Books
SANTA FE, NEW MEXICO

The Polka Dot Chair. Copyright © 2012 by Michele Heeney. All rights reserved. Printed in the United States of America. No part of this book may be used or reproduced in any manner whatsoever without written permission except in the case of brief quotations embodied in critical articles and reviews. Send inquiries to Terra Nova Books, 33 Alondra Road, Santa Fe, New Mexico 87508.

Published by Terra Nova Books, Santa Fe, New Mexico.
www.TerraNovaBooks.com

ISBN 978-1-478304-11-1

Contents

Spirit
Dialogue with Spirit 3
A Drunken Dragonfly 4
Notes From the Borderlands 5
Deep Sea Fishing 6
The Most Beautiful Bird in the World 7
In the Dark 8
The Wind Blows Through Me .9
The Polka Dot Chair 10
Madre de las Estrellas 11
Soul Soup With Biscuits 12
The Philosopher's Stone 13
Meeting the Shadow 14
The Knower and the Known .15
Suspicious Character 16
Why You Came 17

Love
Slow Dance 21
Catch Me 22
Celibacy 23
Standing in Front of Your Door 24
To Run Alone 25
Thoughts South 26
Love Song 27
Cake Dream 28

Time
Night Train 31
Uncharted 32
Miss Behaving 33
Slipping Out 34
Her Past 35
The Last Mayan Calendar 36
Vanishing Vanity 37
Tomorrow 38
On Time 39
A Flight of Hours 40
Two Thieves 41
Time 42

Nature
October 45
Garland of Summer 46
Mount Tamalpais 47
The Faint Scent of Memory 48
Rio Grande 49
Rain 50
Carmel Valley 51
Pirates 52
Spring Drums 53

Art
Poetry 57
Shadow Side 58
Words 59
The Poet 60
Writing 61
Lady Art 62
Dancing the Sky 63

Politics
The U.S.A. 67
Recession's Wedding 68
Two Women 69
Willing Inmates 70
Population Party 71
It Was Your Country 72
Men of Progress 74

Etc.
Furry Worry Monkey 77
Perchance to Dream 78
The Shallow End 79
Maya 80
Fool Moon 81
A Dream 82
Tomatoes and Other Memories 83
The Red Shawl 84
The Scream 85
Squishy 86
Photo Cat 87
Pieces of a Dream 88
Twenty-Three Tears 89
Life 90
Glass Soldier 91

Dedicated to

    All those

        Who dance

            With Spirit

Spirit

Dialogue With Spirit

White hot
Holy spirit

I've felt you
In my body
Through my veins,
With me,
Dazzling me,
Being me.

Where have you gone?

I'm here in the stone wall you built
To keep out blades of cold intellect.

Be Salome.
Have your
Own head
Chopped off,
Breathe through
Your heart.
Then I will
Return to
Set you
Ablaze again.

Drunken Dragonfly

I am the blue black ink
That keeps stars afloat,
I am the endless cosmic night.

I am the life force of every living thing,
I am your blood, your secret heart, your soul.
I am where your spirit goes at death.

I am the measure of wisdom and compassion
And to Whom all religions call,
Though they fail to speak My language.

I write the music of the spheres
And teach the birds to sing it.
I am your prayers answered.

Still, you do not know Me,
Won't catch My name on solar winds
Or hear My voice in ocean waves.

You're like a drunken dragonfly
Ripping off his wings
In flight.

Wake up!
You're missing quite a show.

Notes From the Borderlands

Some of us are wildish
We tear out all the pages
We only roam the borders
Hide the keys to all the cages.

We hear the angels chanting
Know the devil's voices
See the wound in all the wounded
Feel the grief of painful choices.

Some of us live wild
Grow in untamed ways
Love with hearts wide open
Sail uncharted days.

We run across scorched deserts
Dance the highest ledge.
Be careful how you touch us
We walk the sharpest edge.

Some of us are spirit
We dwell in sacred places
We are the shamans to the soul
We own the scars
Seared on our faces.

Deep Sea Fishing

The answer lies
Not in the answer
But hides
In the mystery
Of the question.

Don't search to know,
Search to seek.

In the darkest depths
Of the secret ocean
The rarest
Light shines.

Dive deep,
There lie the treasures
But none to keep.

The Most Beautiful Bird in the World

Could be you,
Ethereal spirit bird,
One wing of wisdom,
One of compassion.

You could fly
On celestial winds
Of non-attachment
Into the golden corona
Of the sacred sun.

Though you will need
Both wings.

In the Dark

Down in the basement
Between silent walls
I learned to see in the dark.

A review of demons
Came floating by.
I learned their names by heart.

No tears, no sighs
Just long, cold stares
From sad, old memories.

While death sat with my shadow,
Ragged regrets chewed on the past
Like ghost cows in the meadow.

Bright colors melted into gray
But with depth and soul
Gray taught.

A sad and chilly place it was
Yet what mystery-gifts
It brought.

Enlightenment in the dark.

The Wind Blows Through Me

Once, I was a wolf
Once, I was the sky
Once, a willow tree.

Time moves
Forms change

Space stays
The same
In me.

Sacred,
Starry,
Wild
And wide.

Space stays
The same
In me.

The Polka Dot Chair

She sat in silence
On the polka dot chair
Waiting for spirit to speak.

He spoke
In a tongue
She did not know,
His voice distant and weak.

He spoke again
So loud, so fierce
The dots fell off
The chair,

"I am your love,
The greatest of loves.
I'm within, I'm without,
And I'll always be there."

Madre de las Estrellas

Santa Maria,
Cosmic feminine of celestial lands
Help her accept the abundant gifts
You have kindly placed in her hands.

Santa Maria,
Mother of the stars above
Let her feel your sweet blessings
Of gratitude and love.

Santa Maria,
May she be permitted
To forgive herself
For sins not committed.

Santa Maria,
Queen of time and space
Hold her up to the moon
That she may kiss its snowy face.

Soul Soup with Biscuits

What must be done
To be real?
What must be done
To be whole?

Simply this:
Be crushed by the weight
Of your own choices,
Wounded by your
Endless labor,

Return to your private journey
A thousand times
Only to fall
A thousand times more.

Marry your fiery heart
To your frozen intellect,
Sit down and eat
Your own raw soul.

Anything less
Isn't real,
Anything less
Isn't whole.

The Philosopher's Stone

When the odyssey
Is over
All the tigers
Tamed,
When there
Is nothing
Left to
Rail against
Except
The wind
The cold
The passing season,

There is still
A lesson waiting
That can change
Lead to stunning gold.

The lesson is
Forgiveness.
The lesson is
The last
And certainly
The hardest.

Meeting the Shadow

As she
Lingers in
The depths
Of soul
She meets
Her fool,
Her failure,
Her sinner.

She walks
Awhile
Among them
Hears their
Stories
Hears their song.

Then grabs
The light
Of self-forgiveness
To fly up
Up and out.

The Knower and the Known

The Great Creator
Wished to know
The joy and agony
Of man,
So He created lovers.

Man wished to know
The mind and purpose
Of God,
So he fell in love.

Suspicious Character

It's not that
God hides out
Only in Jerusalem or Mecca,

Up Sister Mary Michael's sleeve
Or in cumulus clouds,

It's that His essence
Is a bit more dense
In certain geographic areas.

Of course, the infinite cosmos
Has His fingerprints
All over it.

Why You Came

You are
What you are
Here to find.

You are
The treasure
You are seeking.

This crazy labyrinth
You're traveling
Leads inward,

Where you may find
What you have come here
To find.

Love

Slow Dance

Come dance
With me.
Come dance
And be my lover.

Bring red wines
From Argentina
Fine sweets
From Switzerland.

We'll dance
And drink
In golden halls
And when we die
Our dust

Will mingle
To blow across
The surface
Of the earth

Till oceans
Turn to salty mist
And stars
Turn out
Their lights.

Catch Me

Catch me.
Don't let me win this game.
Use your biggest net,
Employ your fastest yacht.
Please, you really ought
To catch me.

If I don't stop soon
I'll run into the moon
Out in cold black space.
What a crazy race.

Grab me by the hand,
Demand I understand
That I'm running out of time.
Lock me in your arms.
Catch me.

If it seems the wind I seek,
It's not. I'm just too weak
To cease this silly game.
What I truly need
Is an end to all this speed.

If, while gazing at the sky,
You see me flying by,
Kiss me on the mouth
    And catch me.

Celibacy

When I knew for certain
No man would soon be near,
I took the angels on.

In that coupling
My heart blew open.
And Beauty
That had been
A stranger to me

Poured forth
Like golden waterfalls.

Standing in Front of Your Door

I once had
A blood red heart,
It sang,
Soared,
Sailed.

Now, it's stuck
To the sole
Of your shoe.

Now, there's a hole
In my chest
Where my heart
Used to be.

So I'm here
At your doorstep
To say,

I want my heart back.

To Run Alone

I am too responsible of late
Keeping needs and hopes behind a heavy gate,
Sending Wonder Girl to run about
Shutting pain and feelings out.

Once in a while my heart breaks through the ice
Of that cold, gray lake it's drowned in twice
And stings me with its hot reality:
You and your love are not here with me.

I run alone so well it just seems right
To give my all on this long, low, solo flight,
But since you've touched me with your face
It seems now a sad and sorry race—

    To run alone.

Thoughts South

Leaving me alone
With your resounding silence
Overwhelms me.

Keeping still,
Not moving,
Engages me entirely.

A slow rope burn
Drags across my chest
Toward my heart.

I'd rather
Fall to hell
And get it over with
Than this.

Love Song

A flutter of emotion
Then sudden flight
On frantic wings.

Freed
From a twice-locked cage
My hopes went flying

To sing silent
Notes of need
Upon your window sill.

Cake Dream

You are a beautiful impossibility,
The road I must not take,

You are a golden angel
A heaven too far,

The red velvet cake
Behind the glass.

Oh, what I'd give
For just one bite!

Time

Night Train

The train
Is empty

My friends
Are gone

I've carelessly
Missed every stop.

There is no
Turning back

The trajectory is
Straight ahead

Alone on an
Empty train

Going God-knows-where
At white hot speed.

Then a Voice,
Not heard but felt:

"You have a choice,
Jump or wait to crash."

Uncharted

My conscious mind
Has its own
Unconscious mind
That rests
On a dark
Uncharted island
That floats on
A collective
Universal sea

Blown about
By hot winds
Born of
Primordial time
Long before
My mind
Met its mind
Or this
Mindful body.

Miss Behaving

South
Of morning
North
Of noon,

East
Of tomorrow
Just west
Of the moon,

Blasting through
The present
In her
Bombastic way

Tearing up
The hours
Back into
Yesterday,

On to
The juncture
Of space
And time,

Will it be
Then, now
Or tomorrow?

Oh, now
She's changing her mind
As well as her mood
And yes,
Even her longitude.

Slipping Out

Who is
At her door
This winter evening?

The fire
So warm
The wine
So sweet.

Who is
Lightly knocking
At her window?

Ah, the three brothers,
Illness, age and death
Knocking gently

While she slips
Softly out the back
With silent breath

Her Past

Is an imaginary quilt
Of about three hundred
Choice patches,
A few thousand
Colored threads.

The sheets
Long since
Gone to tatters,
Then to dust.

The bed frame?
Well, it no longer
Stands at all.

The Last Mayan Calendar

Those amusing
Little Mayans
They sure have
A sense of humor
To start this
Crazy, grand,
This extraordinary
Rumor.

Now we're
All running scared
While they just
Wink and grin.

Don't be
A silly rooster
The sky's not
Falling in.

Don't fret
My friend
The world's not
Coming to an end.

They just stopped making calendars.

Vanishing Vanity

First
I go
To crepe

Then
I go
To dust

Then
I go
To ether.

I think
That while
In ether

I will not wear
My pretty
Diamond ring.

Tomorrow

We are day-eaters all,
Gluttons of time,
Mindlessly taking in
Morsels of moments
That will be served
But once.

Tomorrow we'll drink
A bitter brew
Of stale regrets
To clear our mouths
And minds
Of those half-tasted
Yesterdays.

On Time

Time is
Most pleasant
When I
Forget
Its passing,

When the
Ticking on
The wall
Evaporates,

When I look
Up from thought
Or action
To find the hours
Have melted,

Along with
My need
To measure
Them.

A Flight of Hours

In the day
Before tomorrow
In the year before
The next

Pay attention
To your hours
Or you may
Find yourself
In the desolate forest
Of pale memories

Where if you dwell
Too long
Time brings you to
The end of
All tomorrows.

Pay close attention
To the hours
Of today,

For unlike
Robins in spring,
They do not
Fly home again.

Two Thieves

Age steals youth,
Death steals more.
Age dusts the windows,
Death shuts the door.

Age takes beauty,
Death, hope of spring,
Age takes laughter,
Death, everything.

Age steals thoughts
And times once known,
Age takes memories,
Death leaves its own.

Age knows good times,
Death knows none.
Age takes many,
Death, everyone.

Time

Willowy aftermath
Of half-remembered dreams.

Gossamer mist dividing
Today from forever.

We watch our hours
From a door beyond,

To pass through
In silken slippers.

Nature

October

October sings a haunting song
Of chilly days and frosted nights,
Yet she gaily goes along
In resplendent robes
Of red and golden lights.

Summer's past her prime,
Still she charms with all the force
Of her adolescent way,
Through the meadows and the farms
Filled high with harvest
Where all the season's treasures lay.

October hums an ancient tune
That tells of fear and dread,
Beneath her autumn sky
Of bright stars
And harvest moon
She has a dagger hidden
In her glowing gown of red.

She shivers hard and long
Causing cold bones,
Dark nights to splinter.
She shudders with a chill so strong
For she knows that all too soon
She'll have to sleep
With winter.

Garland of Summer

Heart breakable star-drenched sky
Velvet black in deep July,
My blood turns to honey wine
Warmed by the breath
Of ocean winds that drift
Through tall and flaxen wheat
On waves of summer heat.

Our skin turns pink, then peach, then tan,
Sweet apricot juice stains
My shirt and hand
While your hair is blown about
Like wild corn silk in the breeze.

Sweet July and August
Run together, and soon
We feel as young as any
Yearling doe beneath the moon
Grazing on fallen plums at night.

All but forgotten
Cold February's chill,
Month of brittle bones
And frozen dawns
Without the bright orange sun's good will.

Stay, O warm July.
Please linger long.
Too soon
Comes the weight
Of winter's crushing wheel
When wine turns again to blood
And bones to steel.

Mount Tamalpais

Weary of wishing
Soft lay me down,
Spent of ambition
On your cool ground.

High mother mountain
On you I rest,
Peace from your fountain
I drink from your breast.

Cradle me sweetly
As I sleep by your streams
Humbly I seek thee
To nourish old dreams.

The Faint Scent of Memory

The pale
Blossoms of
My cherry tree
Bloom just
Outside
The gate.

Magically
Their sweet scent
Rides on the wind
Long before
The first few
Buds appear.

Rio Grande

Clouds alive
With mist
And wind

Dance through
The branches
Of the cottonwoods.

The Rio Grande
Caresses their reflection.

A scattershot
Of swallows
Blow about
Like black confetti.

The banks
That hold the river
Breathe silent prayers
Of stillness,

As the river sings
Her autumn song.

Rain

As spring
Rain
Melts
Winter
Ice,

Living
Wears away
Thoughts
Of
You.

Carmel Valley

That restless
Soul of mine
Finally slipped
Its silver anchor
Over the side,

Deep into that
Green and golden
Patch of earth.

I, of course,
Kept roaming
Through other
Charming lands

While my soul,
Still tethered
To the anchor,
Stayed.

Pirates

A chorus of
One hundred
Blackbirds
Screech
Scream
And scold
Whenever
I near the tree.

I am
Chief Rival
For the choice
Fallen walnuts,

A bounty of
Tiny
Well-locked
Treasure chests.

Spring Drums

I hear
The drumming
From the sky,
From deep

Beneath the earth
Slowly, louder
Reaching for
My ears.

Drumming
The inner me
A familiar call
A high desert song:

Come out
Come out and
Dance with me
Through the mesa
Among the juniper
Over the Jemez
Into wilder parts.

Come out
Old girl
Come out
And dance

Earth
Has turned
Away from
Winter.

Art

Poetry

When writing
As with living
It's often best
To be still,
To wait,
To listen
For the right words
The right meaning
That lives not
In the mind
But in the bones.

When lost in confusion
And leaning too close
To logic
Trust that the light
Will find you
That mystery will
Solve itself.

Trust in fruition
Where beauty and form
Will materialize
From a deeper,
Untamed region.

Pushing, pulling,
Beating on the door
Only leads us
Off the scent
Where only
Stillness and letting go
Will see us home.

Shadow Side

Where is my dark poet,
The seeker of shadow,
The reader of dreams?

Where is my night angel
Who watches at evening
As the blackbird sleeps,

Knows where the rabbits run
As the nighthawk hunts,
How the river holds the moonlight?

Where is my secret self
Who flashes golden spurs at dawn?

Then gone!

Words

Bright, exotic
Butterflies
With pretty
Colored wings

Now and then
Alight upon
The paper.

Though they arrive
In spider's
Sticky web

Or crimson
Belgian lace,

We accept
Delivery.

The Poet

Papers,
Pens,
Memory sticks,

Impromptu romps
Through hell
To muse awhile
With Psyche.

One thousand
Sequestered hours
To simmer,
Dream,
Remember.

All this
To risk parting
The curtains,
If only for a moment,
To risk being known,
If only to herself.

Writing

Only seems
A lonely task.

A host of
Spirits
Gather

To help me
Move the pen.

Lady Art

Often wears
A filmy wrap
That veils
Her hidden meaning,

Yet through
A tiny pinhole
In her gown
The artist's
Inner spark
Is sought
And found,

A moment more,
The pinhole's
Doubly sewn.
Yet for one
Speck of time
The sensual form
Is fully known.

Dancing the Sky

Intrepid little dancer
Blasts onto the stage

Spinning into space,
Slipping gravity's sticky grip.

A slash of lightning
Slicing through the stratosphere,

Dancing the sky.

While we earthbound stay,
Lusting after flight.

Dancing down the heights
Through a thunder of applause
The little dancer
Gently lands back
On Earth again.

Politics

The U.S.A.

When truth
Becomes false
False true

When up
Is down
Down up

The house may
Spontaneously combust

Sending us all
Running for
Far Canada.

Recession's Wedding

I'll buy the whiskey
I'll make the bread,

I'll wash the sheets
For the wedding bed.

A grand day it will be
The day we wed.

And you, my love,
Bring stones for soup.

Two Women

She said
   No
To two
   Yes
To one.

That's why
Her story sounds
So strange to you.

You said
   No
To the wide highway,
   Yes
To the comfort train.

That's why
Your story sounds
So odd to her.

She chose
The call of
The unconscious wilderness
Not the lure
Of hearth and home.

That's why
She's still discussing
The joy and cost
Of freedom
With a thousand angels
On the mountain's
Rocky edge.

Willing Inmates

You're never going
Where I have been.

What I have seen
You'll never see.

What I know
You can't imagine.

You may have more
But more is not enough.

Do you ever listen
To the wisdom on the wind?

Do you lift one foot
To journey down your own path?

The prison bars around your mind
You've forged yourself.

Will a hundred lifetimes come and go
Before you simply open the door
And leave the cell?

Population Party

The table's full
To overflowing.
They sit between
The chairs.

Scant food is
In the kitchen.
They're fighting on the stairs.

The place in tatters,
We can't invite
One person more.

Yet there's five
Hundred thousand
Still standing
At the door.

Someone please
Tear up the invitations.
This party's over.

It Was Your Country

I know you've yet to find
The words to
Hold the feeling.

So, let me say it for you.

The truth and beauty
Of the dream
Was real to you.

The dream was yours.
You held the key.
It was your country.

And now?

You are a useless
Clay container,
Emptied out.

It's over.

The jackals have won.
Of course they won.
You didn't know
You were the enemy.

They're sucking on your bones.
They're eating your children.
The blood is on the walls.

They used your dreams.
Dreams that are
Just a foolish memory.

You're no longer needed.
They wish you'd walk
Out into space
And disappear.

Ninety nine plus one
Now equals one.

So, have I said it right?
Have I said it well
enough?

Men of Progress

Please don't
Blow up
The moon

We have
Grown quite
Fond of her.

The tides
Of oceans,
The tides
Of our bodies
Have fallen in love
With her magic
Push and pull.

Her light
In the night sky,
The hope
In darkness
And foreboding,
The play
Of form and change,
The silver pendant
The ancients
Have passed down.

Leave the moon
To her eternal birth.
Haven't you done enough
To Earth?

Furry Worry Monkey

That monkey's back again.

Jumps on my head,
Bangs into Buddha,
Jangles joy,
Pushes over peace,
Slices up silence.

I tell that monkey,
"We've plowed this field
Ten thousand times."

That monkey don't care,
Keeps on plowing.

Finally he's kaput,
Leaps off my head,
Jumps out the window.

That crazy monkey!

Perchance to Dream

Slowly slipping
Into the silent
Stream of sleep,
Sinking softly
Into quicksand
Half an acre deep.

Leaving sticky tangles
Far behind,
Toward the arms
Of vast unconscious bliss,
Letting go
The restless,
Racing mind.

Traveling down
The edge
Of the indigo abyss.

Down, down
Once again
To kiss
The constant lover,
Sweet Morpheus.

The Shallow End

He chases
His senses
Down life's
Grand corridor,

Forgetting spirit,
Blocking mind,
Dishonoring body,

Letting his senses
(Five drunken monkeys)
Take the lead.

I watch him
Trip, fall, bleed
On his path of
Sensuality,

Missing all
The signs,
Dismissing all
The warnings.

I watch as he
Chases pleasure
Down a pier
Long and wide

Races straight
Off the end

Into the churning tide.

Maya

One day
He had a thought
He fell in love with.

His thought
Became a belief
He turned into
A glowing pearl.

He placed the pearl
On an ebony stand,
Placed the stand
In a tiny palace.

He worshipped
His belief
Suffered and
Bled for it

Until the moment
He awoke from illusion
To see his sacred,
Beautiful thought,
His precious pearl,
Was wrong.

In that instant
The pearl became
A diamond.

Fool Moon

This big full moon
Takes hold of me
Won't set me free
Till the end of night.

That bright orb hanging,
Keeps my brain clanging,
Gets strange ghosts banging,
Like old barn doors.

This big full moon
With its neon grin
Takes me by the throat,
Lets the night witch in.

That cool moon glow
With ice blue light
Takes hold of me
Till the end of night,

Till the dawn.

A Dream

In my dream
I heard "Divest."
I watched my
Hand let go
Of all my
Worldly treasures
From my worldly
Treasure chest.

Then, just before
Reaching for the door,
The door to eternity,

I stood naked
And luminous
With fantastic
Golden wings.

Tomatoes and Other Memories

What's up
With tomatoes
Anyway?

They tasted
Like heaven
In their day.

But now they
Taste more or less
Like hay,

And they cost
A whole lot more.

The Red Shawl

From time
To time,
Quietly
Disguised as
Ordinary,
Peace comes
To call,

Wafts in
On sweet
Scented
Incense,

Shyly slips
A soft
Red shawl
Around my
Shoulders.

Then,
Just as I
Speak her name,
As would a startled sparrow
Peace departs.

The Scream

A sharp red sliver
Of a long high scream
Cut the black silk night
To ribbons.

With that, I knew
The night
And scream
Were mine,
Black silk ribbons
And all.

Squishy

The turtle,
Oyster,
Snail,
All have their shell

The porcupine
Its quills

The rhino
Has its armor

The dog
Its teeth
That may
Bite you
As you pass.

But I'm no armadillo
I walk about
This earth
With just
A pair of jeans
To save my squishy ass.

Photo Cat

My cat
Does not
Like her
Picture taken.

She prefers traveling
This world
Unseen by many

Quietly padding
About with
Little fanfare.

Immortality
Is not
Her game.

Pieces of a Dream

Humming
A fragment
Of lost melody.

Once again
Wishing
To reconstruct
The song
That stays
Just out
Of reach.

All that's left,
A pale
Memory
Of last
Night's dream

That rises
For an instant,
A moment later—
Descends again.

Twenty-Three Tears

Swallow back
Too many tears
You get
Streams,
Rivers,
Oceans.

Avoid drowning,
Cry a little
So that simple sorrow
Does not turn
To frothing seas,
Pitching waves,
Or deep, black whirlpools
To pull you down
To a watery floor.

Life

Not how long
Not how well
But how deep.

Not how far
You've come
But how far
From where
You started.

Glass Soldier

Sent out
In glory
And speeches

Returns home
In broken
Jagged pieces.

Why write
Of such sorrow
From our past?

Because
We all are soldiers
Made of glass.

About the Author

For many years, Michele Heeney's life was centered around giving birth in the literal sense, as an obstetrics and gynecology nurse practitioner. But at the same time, her creativity in the more-personal sense also was flourishing: "I was always writing poetry and taking pictures."

Now that the medical world has shifted into the past for her, the poetic and visual arts have leaped to the fore, producing images of striking beauty as well as her new fourth book of poetry, *The Polka Dot Chair*. And throughout this artistic journey, as both bodies of work powerfully declare, has run the unifying thread of Michele's deep love for nature.

After working as an RN in western Pennsylvania, where she was born and raised, she found her vision opened up to a changing world by the energy of San Francisco and the '60s. California became her new home, with an expanded career as an OB/GYN nurse practitioner. What followed was a time of rewarding work in both professional and human terms, first for Planned Parenthood and later for a county hospital serving a large population of Mexican farm workers.

"I would drive through the fields near Salinas and see my patients there," Michele says. "It was extremely interesting. I loved it. I felt I touched people."

In addition to the personal closeness her job brought during this time, nature filled her life at home—a 6,000-acre ranch at the north end of the Big Sur wilderness where she was caretaker for the regional park district that operated it.

These are the links that informed her work, and travel over the years completed the chain. West Africa with the Peace Corps, learning Spanish in Costa Rica, scuba diving in Fiji and Micronesia—just a few of the many places whose experiences merge today to feed Michele's imagination and gift for lyric imagery.

Her perspective and emotion lend a special voice to this wide-ranging path. Her book's sections—Spirit, Love, Time, Nature, Art, Politics—are concerns never far from any of our minds. And Michele's vivid words and thoughts bring us the gift of a unique new perspective on these eternal themes.

Made in the USA
San Bernardino, CA
05 July 2014